Trauma into Truth
Gutsy Healing and Why It's Worth It

Table of Contents

Introduction

My definition of Healing; to make whole, to mend the soul, to come to know and experience one's own innate goodness.

I am an artist.
I am a healer.
I am a therapist.
I am a dancer.
I am a dedicated peace maker.

This is a book about healing and what that word means. I speak from my own full-bodied experience of wild, unkempt discoveries of becoming whole. Coming to terms with my past over the last fifteen years has tested my every resource. I have landed in a beautiful space where now I sit and listen to others and it does not scare me. Sometimes I am saddened, even shocked by what people have lived through but I am consistently touched by the courage and liveliness that comes forward to heal a soul.

Trauma can be any event that feels life threatening to a person. Loss, displacement, illness, neglect, physical, emotional, or sexual abuse can manifest pathways of extreme confusion and fear. So many children and adults live through terrifying events but do not get the chance to process, unravel, or mend that pain.

This book is about completing unfinished business. My intention is to encourage you to do the work of remembering and healing because it is worth the goods. So much good. Huge goodness and joy is waiting in that same psychic box that says "Keep Out."

I set for myself the task of answering questions about healing from trauma asked by clients, friends, and family over the years. These are questions I have also asked myself and answered through writing, dancing, singing, performing, and painting. I painted the images on these pages during years of intensive healing as a way to connect with and express my essential intact self, sometimes during very dark days. The process of making art became my prayer.

My hope is to spark that place in you with my words and art so that we can walk together on this "path less traveled." We have all suffered hurts and we all deserve to be loved through what is unresolved. Healing is an untamed spiritual journey, one that leads straight to who you are. Let's go there.

What is healing?

Healing is the small voice that pierces your sleep and will not let you slumber until you've listened. It calls you towards an opening of unknown origin. It lures you to a brittle edge and asks you to jump.

Healing is the memory of your child eyes looking out at people and things without protection. Your tender wrists. Your hopeful visions.

Healing will ask you to crawl through muck like a soldier, through fields of demons and horrors beyond your wildest imagination. It will call you to blackness.

You may slip between a crack in the Earth and fall. You may find yourself covered in heavy awareness, unable to breathe. The sounds may be deafening, your body screaming. You may believe you are losing the world, all your loved ones, your sanity, your identity.

Healing is merciful and will not leave you alone. True healing has hands of potent beauty. It wakes you to your deepest knowing and will not let you forget your core. Healing is the light at the end of the tunnel and the next tunnel and the next. Each time you will rise like a cloud higher and higher in the sky of compassion. You will come to know your goodness despite the lies. You will find yourself standing on solid legs of truth. If your intention is to heal, I believe you can.

What does healing look like?

First I had nightmares, then insomnia. They alternated. I was nauseous, then starving. My body was battered, constantly remembering, and then it would open. My friends were my band aids, my angels, then they were monsters. I saw the Universe in two halves, the Now and the Then.

Now I was making marks of integrity on the Earth's surface, a functioning adult. Then I was breaking into bits, small and defenseless, a little girl without choices. I lived a double life, working during the day, smiling, talking, paying bills. At any given pause, I was vacuumed back in time to images of angry faces and unseeing hands, my child body taken hostage by people I trusted most. During the day, I was a dancer capable of great freedom, moving my limbs in ecstatic articulations. At night, I covered my body parts with my palms, curled up, shook.

For a while, healing was ugly, massive, chalky, crinkled, rude, and explosive. It spit me out onto shores beyond all living things. I felt like a reptile in a land of mammals. Eventually Then and Now made bridges. Separate realities of danger and safety came close within me. I could straddle them both and not live in one or the other. I could hold turbulent memory in the hearth of my present-day peace.

I came to be one whole thing; a being of what-actually-happened integrated with what-actually-is. I looked and felt alive with emotion and knowledge, and I was. My life had grown from insurmountable pain into purposeful awakened resonance.

LEARN TO TRUST YOUR WINGS...

Where's the joy?

Are you kidding? Joy is the whole point! Joy is the reward of facing the real down and dirty truth. You know that expression, "the only way out is through?" It refers to the transformational process of embracing pain in order to get to liberation. Well, healing is like running a marathon.

The race starts slow, the body is stiff yet you feel as if you can do anything. You break into a stride, falling into motion, the rhythm of your breath opening your senses. Your bones are solid, you almost glide. Gradually, resistance starts to build, fear creeps in, you notice you're slowing down. The doubt collides with the effort and you start to think maybe you can't make it. Smack in the middle of the race, a hurricane hits you full force. You're sure your limbs are being scattered over North America, but you keep running, running, running. The finish line is lit up in your mind like a Zeppelin. You emerge from the storm shaken, exhausted, undone but you see the end in sight, you're still running. Every last step feels like a year of your life. Still you run. You run and you step. You step over that finish line and something snaps in your brain. You are far more powerful then you ever imagined. Your heart is beating loud and clear, your muscles are filled with blood. You look around and the trees are so bright, you feel as if you might cry. Your friends are all around clapping and cheering. You see your strength in their eyes. Suddenly, you know that half way through the marathon you shed the part of you that was separate from God, the part that was covered in a heavy coat of shame. You saw that wool shroud in pieces on the road and the person who had run onward, the person who you always were.

Is healing about rebellion?

We are all programmed, fed images and thought forms. There is so much programming that we don't even notice it most of the time. There are levels of it, lies that block our authentic ways of being in the world, and lies that can ultimately destroy us.

In my work as a counselor, I have found that most trauma survivors have internalized the belief that something is inherently wrong with them. When it comes to childhood abuse, core shame often gets created and children come to believe they are profoundly damaged. They grow up to be adults who hide their shame through addictions, tumultuous relationships, or through quiet self-hatred that infiltrates various aspects of their lives. One major false belief such as "I am unlovable" can threaten an entire life.

So, there is a kind of rebellion in taking the time to dissect what we have been taught. There is a certain level of standing apart from our parents and family, our teachers, our government, our friends, the media, even from ourselves. This investigation cannot be done on an intellectual level. It must be resolved through the emotional body and fed into a deeper spiritual questioning. It can be a challenging path, but because it births truth, it is also very exhilarating.

To truly grow up, to become an adult, one has to spend the time asking the hard questions of what it meant to have lived through one's own life. What hurt, what felt good, what moments compromised your integrity, how do they still? In a way, it is easier to be a programmed person, to follow some kind of norm, to repeat what was passed on to your body, mind, and heart. There is a rebellion in the act of growing conscious and becoming an individual in the truest sense of the word.

How does the heart speak?

My friend Samantha said to me this morning, "Ambiguity is the stuff of life." She gave me a big hug in the middle of the kitchen. I'd been musing about my recent breakup with a man who had been pushing me to my edge. The breakup had lasted a week and a half and then we had stayed up until three in the morning talking it through.

Black or white? Black or white? My mind screamed about love. Yes or no? Good or bad? Right or wrong? The child inside me broke it all down. Mom was good, Dad was bad. I was wrong, they were right. My friends were perfect, I was defective. The act of hanging out in a mess was unknown. To stay in a place of confusion reminded me of my little girl bed and the cavern in my heart that got made there. Black or white were islands I could jump onto when things were breaking.

As an adult, meditation saved me. Sitting in the space below thoughts, the "being" place, has settled my hyper-vigilant heart. In the still hush of time, the beating sound is wordless. I am led by a quiet thrust of knowledge towards an open alleyway of mercy. Underneath the stories I made up about all my deficiencies is my undeniable humane heart almost laughing, willing to take on the challenge of loving another human being. There, that tender uncomplicated state of acceptance breathes despite the crushing that came before. Red, raw, ambiguous heart turning my life inside out.

Aren't you angry?

     I used to have this small singing voice. Very pinched. I had great enthusiasm but couldn't get any volume. The year I started having traumatic flashbacks, I was living alone. My apartment was basically underground, a spiffed up basement. I began my healing process literally holed up.

     I had nightmares of childhood sexual abuse vivid as firecrackers. I would wake up screaming with my bones twisted in some inhuman position. Sometimes the injustice of what happened to me would hit me so hard, I would bolt out to my car and get inside. I would drive my blue Volkswagen out to some deserted street and turn on the radio full blast. Then, once the windows were rolled up tight, I would holler with all my might every obscenity I could think of, punching the roof of my car with my fists. "!@#$*&%@$#!!!!" My aim was to break the sound barrier, scream the shame off my skin. I would yell until my voice was hoarse, my body exhausted and then I would cry. Out

17

among the trees, with the wind blowing hard, with the sound of the river not far away, with various songs ringing in my ears, I would weep for myself. Helplessness would vibrate through my chest and heart.

I began this car screaming ritual at the beginning of 1997. By the end of that summer, I could sing like a bird, a very loud bird, strong and on pitch belting out "God Bless the Child" into oblivion. All that cursing had cleared a path from my gut to my vocal chords. A channel had opened because I was angry and had let it be ok.

Was it lonely?

Lonely like a solitary walk down a long wooded pathway. Lonely like the sting of cold air when your warm hand lets go of mine. Lonely as if I am entering a park full of busy unrecognizable people. I have felt this sweet kind of lonely.

Then there was the lonely of sitting across the dinner table looking at my mother and sensing something was wrong. A wall, an electric fence, a city of buildings, an entire continent between us. She had hurt me early on but now she was smiling at me. Her arms had not held me when I was tiny and crying but now she smiled at me as if we were close. I told myself lies in order to feel one with her. I said she would never hurt me, she didn't mean to, it never happened, I'm crazy, and clearly we are close, look at how her eyes water when she smiles at me. I created vats of fantasies setting off warm fuzzies within me, living inside them completely.

All the fantasies in the world could not eradicate my terror. That kind of loneliness was deadly. The loneliness of sitting across from someone who supposedly adores you and feeling sheer terror. That kind of loneliness would undo me. So I went away and learned to live with a lonely that had congruence. I was alone, I was without the woman who had given birth to me. I was leaping into a void of unknown solitude but I could live with that loneliness. It was a lonely that made sense.

Is healing a selfish act?

There have been countless days when I wanted my life to be different. I wanted my parents to be different parents, my siblings to be different siblings, my path to be a different path. I went so far as to pretend the abuse I suffered did not exist. I was willing to blot out any inkling of unrest just to have a family, to be part of the only home I had ever known.

Was it selfish to choose the truth above all else, even security? Was it selfish to dive into years of grief and longing to give birth to the only self available to me, me?

Selfish would have been passing the abuse on to my children, my loved ones, my partner. Selfish would have been carrying the denial into the next generation. Selfish would have been becoming an angry, scared, small, withheld person who never healed, who did not find her clear unique voice.

If I did not choose to remember the violence, the sexual abuse, the loss, the crazy-making epicenter of my childhood, I would not know who I am. I would not have harbored the tools of self-responsibility that enabled me to be in service to other survivors. I would not have grasped, down to the bone, the kind of atrocities people live through and been able to offer my understanding.

The time it has taken to recover my essence has been a long, indescribably challenging road. I wanted to skip the journey and go into hiding. I craved addictions and self-destructive acts that would turn off the stark reality of what people do to children. But then, in the quiet place of faith, I sensed that love was growing. Every day it grew in the compost of my terror. Amidst the wreckage of what people call "The American Family" stood a figure unafraid. I had something to give and it had not died.

What does your story have to do with healing?

My story is just one story. I could tell it in a breath: I was born, the people I loved hurt me, I thought it was my fault, and realized much much later that it wasn't.

Or I lost myself. I had to give up knowing who I was in order to get attention, approval, safety. I thought I was that manufactured person, but found much later, a beaten but tenacious soul relentlessly clearing her throat.

Or life shaped me like a rock spinner, so much shock and slam, harsh, cutting lessons. It seemed I was breaking up, becoming dirt beneath the weight of heavy objects, like grand pianos and air conditioners. I found out much later, I was not broken, just dizzy.

The main point of my life story is to be a reminder to myself (and maybe to others) that I am not my life story and never was. It is a part of me. It illustrates the darkest of human behavior, the ultimate lightness of human recovery, but that is all. Moment to moment, I am something else all together. This awareness is what healing graciously holds out to me, even as I pick up my story again and again, and then put it down.

How has art saved you?

Art is the juice of life! The oil that makes the motor run. The spiritual blood that fills the shell of a strong body. Creativity is the four pronged plug that when hooked up to God, lights the sky and all the surrounding trees.

As a child, I see myself with magic markers in each hand drawing colors on the page while my family buzzed around me. I could retreat into a sparkling place where every line, circle, scribble, meant I existed. My tender mind could lose itself in tactile bliss, secretly forming pathways to an unspeakable solace.

I see myself as a ten year old, desperately lonely, searching for the will to live once my body was in motion. When I discovered dance, it was as if a lighted path became suddenly visible. I was taken by the power of spontaneous choreography. If I entered just the right doorway, I was cata-pulted into a timeless pleasure no one had ever told me about, a place where both my feet could touch the ground without punishment. I danced alone across the purple rug of my bedroom, all lanky arms and legs, to vinyl records of Billy Joel. I remember an instant of spiritual connection so intense and complete that the world was forever changed. As life dealt me a hand of unpredictable challenge, there was the unconscious knowledge of a way out.

Art is still my bread and butter, my diamond in the rough, my Queen Bee. Writing, drawing, dancing, singing, painting, playing guitar, performing- take these pearls away and life is flat, flat, flat. But it is more than that. It is about giving voice and form to a benevolent mystery. During the darkest of times, through the ecstasy of my evolvement, art has become the unconditional home that waits with open arms.

Who heals?

A remarkable aspect of being a therapist is giving assistance to those who ask. When a person is ready, they will utilize every tool I offer, transform under my gaze, heal themselves just like a self-cleaning oven! But when they are not ready, or when my presence is not what is needed, there is absolutely nothing I can do to ease the pain. I can only trust that healing will come in their time, in ways I may or may not be a part of.

When I stand in front of a person who feels broken, who has left his or her body long ago, I become a witness. I aim to show pathways toward divinity. I hold a space of unconditional love that does not assume to know how that person's path should unfold.

What I have seen is that a person's choice to reconnect to his or her truth will wake that person up. Healing begins when becoming a loving person to one's self and to others is the foremost priority; more than making money, more than

MOTHER CHILD DREAM SWEET SAFE IN A PURE WORLD WHERE LOVE IS A LIGHT THAT NEVER GOES OUT AND HOLDS THEM AS ONE.

looking good, more than controlling what other people think, more than pleasing one's parents, more than escaping emotion. It is the counter-culture choice to put healing first. Who makes that choice and how it is made is beyond my understanding. I am just blessed to be part of the inquiry.

Do you feel at home in your body?

Sexual abuse is a complex form of violence. Shame gets passed down from abuser to victim through acts of violation and manipulation. The body who receives the assault will remember the terror and helplessness even if the mind blocks it out. The betrayal is carried in the cells waiting to be talked about, understood, and resolved.

After living through a childhood of severe sexual abuse, it has been a long journey back to a loving connection to my body. The abuse created a body, mind, and spiritual confusion that took years to unravel. When you add the wide spread cultural objectification of women on top of how I was violated, it is incredible to me that I found my way back.

I spent years of my adulthood seeing myself as a compilation of flaws. Nothing came out right- my eyes, my skin, all my features were wrong. Oh, and my figure was too everything and not enough of everything else! It took some time but I came to understand that to believe myself beautiful felt like an invitation for harm. I sensed a little girl inside me who did not feel safe being pretty. My self-criticism was my protection.

Once I truly grasped that the abuse was not my fault, it made all the difference. I discovered what mattered and what did not matter about looks and image. I felt the essence beneath the form.

Now, I can love my body for surviving. I love it for eating, sleeping, talking, breathing... the simple things. When it hurts, I slow down and listen. When it tires, I grow still. When it burns with passion, of course, I dance. My body can still express itself and for that I am deeply thankful.

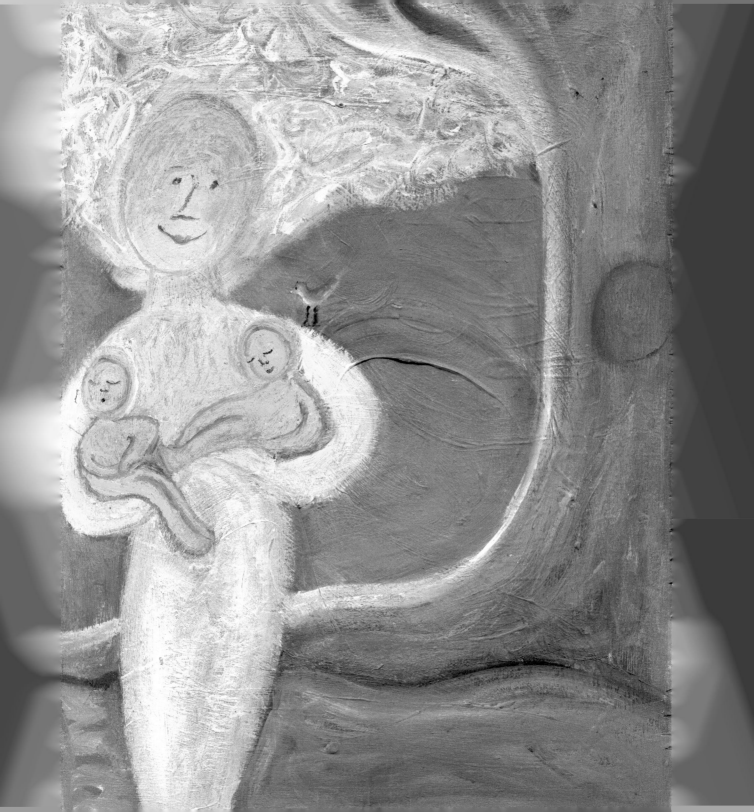

What about sex?

The daring question. Healing sexuality. It is something about putting love back into the word sex. Bringing sex and love together again; the angels who wandered off; introducing them, like old friends separated very young; like lifelong colleagues who think alike; like two saints who need each other's wisdom to teach an ancient doctrine.

Sexuality is one of the most wonderful, exuberant expressions of aliveness. The way it gets warped in this world sheds light on a misunderstanding of the sacred. There is nothing quite like the marriage of heart and body with another person whom you truly adore. If healing is worth nothing else, it is to experience this openness.

If the heart is blocked, the body is blocked. If the channel to one's true nature has not been found, then sexuality is only a glimpse of brilliant color. Trauma of any kind can become this barricade and rob people of their birthright, which is an innocent kind of embodiment.

Healing sexuality is part of healing all other aspects of self. It feeds into the same river. If people dive into their fears and hammer away at their misconceptions of "badness" or "wrongness," the light will break through all the layers. One core layer is sexuality and it will be healed as part of a much bigger whole. Once the flow begins, there is an ocean waiting.

Who are your witnesses?

I found an enlightened witness when I was most unnerved. She looked quite normal but she had this unusual capacity to let me unravel. I came apart somewhat dramatically and it was almost as if she smiled because she knew I was coming together. But she didn't smile, she made a space so large and quiet that when she spoke, it reverberated into my suspicion. She was unafraid and that was a gift.

It has become clear to me through the years that anyone can become a therapist. Anyone can go to graduate school, graduate with a degree, obtain a license, and saddle up with some top-notch theories. Anyone can charge a bundle, sit on a wicker chair and look interested. I've met some of these anyones.

My first official therapist assisted me in retrieving a repressed memory, rallied me through the grueling process of naming the face of my tormentor, and then announced that she didn't believe me. After devastating consequences, I came to learn that she did this with her clients as a regular practice. How lovely!

I swore off therapy for life but then in desperation began interviewing professionals like a mad woman. The process of asking questions and screening down the finalists lead me to a single question posed to each candidate, "Have you done your own healing?" Out of a large number of therapists, one woman told me then and there that a healer cannot heal unless she has healed herself first. Over many years of rock solid support, she proved to me how true that statement was.

Rvthea Lee

What about when people say that trauma survivors should just "get over it?"

I wish it could be that easy. I wish getting over it meant ignoring our past and then "Voila" no more addictions, no more psychic complications, no more physical manifestations of memory, no more neurotic replays of dysfunctional situations. How wonderful it could be if we could just blot out our bummer stories, go to Disneyland, and ride the gargantuan water slide off into the sunset. That would be fabulous.

I wish someone could tell me to get over it (as many do in their shrouded, scared way) and that would hit a magic spot in my brain and then I really was over it, just like that. Even better, what if I could tell my clients to get over it and they did, in fifteen minutes or less. True, I would be out of a job pretty quickly, but it would be worth it just to see so many spontaneous cures.

It is a cultural reality that we are bombarded with the

message "get over it." Taking responsibility for our own joy and peace by mending our histories is not a mainstream practice. Most people are ignoring the pain inside and that is why addictions are needed. You can "get over" old hurts by drinking, eating, or obsessively falling in love. There are people who use meditation or religion to "get over it," attempting a spiritual bypass. But it doesn't work. The pain and the joy are in the same box. If you skip the pain, you don't get the joy either.

Does surviving trauma make intimate relationships difficult?

Most people harbor a trauma or two they hope to never reveal lest their lover think them permanently damaged. The media brainwashes us into thinking if we just find the right partner, we'll be safe, peaceful, and fulfilled. If we knew that getting into relationship actually meant engaging in a stew of our unresolved secrets and pain, would we even do it? And how many people really do it? How many couples use their relationship to grow spiritually by triggering then embracing old wounds in each other?

One thing is for sure, intimate relationships require us to feel helpless. We can't control what our partners think, feel, say, want, or do. How they eat, drink, sleep, who their friends are, if they go to therapy, what they work on in therapy, if they love us all the time, sometimes, or hardly ever. We have no control over their love!

For a trauma survivor, reliving helplessness is not a

pretty prospect. People will push, pull, withdraw, blame, manipulate, cry, yell, drink, act out, whatever it takes to not feel helpless over another person. It is too familiar. It conjures up memories of being children and not being able to get our needs met, to be kept safe, to be truly seen. So we try to make it happen now with our partners, hoping if we try hard enough (i.e., control) it will come out different this time.

Each one of us has to learn about taking care of ourselves and allowing the ones we love to be who they are. That does not mean being silent or passive. It means acting from compassion. In the end, we can only heal ourselves, give from our fullness, and hope to be met deeply on the journey of letting go.

How do you know if you are healed?

Someone recently said to me "You don't have to heal, we are all already healed." I thought to myself, "Well, that's a nice little stocking stuffer but I happen to live on planet Earth. Maybe this looks like a healed Utopia to you, but I've got an acupuncture appointment to keep." Perhaps, in the broadest philosophical sense, at the highest spiritual level, he was right. Possibly I am perfect and there is nothing to look at, explore, cry about, rage about, remember, or forget. There is truth to that. But it has been a process of overhauling my operating system to get to the place where I live from my truth. For me, healing is a life long undertaking where the demons tackled are rewarded with larger amounts of freedom. I was giving an interview for a newspaper about my dance theater company that performs on the subject of healing. The interviewer asked, "So where does all this expression leave you? I mean, after 12 years of performing and teaching professionally, are you healed?" I was stunned by the question. Am I healed? I stammered inside, could I be healed? Then I found myself saying, "Yes, I am. My history no longer dictates how I live my life or how I feel about myself." I smiled because some evolved part of me had answered the question.

I still hurt, I still struggle, I still have inner mulch to make art about (relationships, politics, potato chips), but now there is a place I tap into that is absolutely independent of my wounds and sufferings. The process of coming to full-bodied grips with my past has tipped the scales from unconscious reactions to a reality that moves from a deeper unscarred knowing. This is my evidence that there is rhyme and reason to dismantling our false beliefs, getting to the bottom of our self blame.

When I looked back at my life, at the lowest
and saddest points, there were only one set
of footprints in the sand. I asked the Goddess
how she could have abondoned me at those
times when I needed her most. The Goddess
replied, "My precious, precious child, I love you
and would never leave you during your times
of trial and suffering. When you see only one
set of footprints, it was then that **I carried you**."

What if I don't want to remember what it was like to be a child?

You were a baby, you were a toddler, you were a young child, a teenager, a budding adult. On a physiological level, you remember it all. Each moment is stored somewhere in your brain, every cough, whisper, and breath, whether you consciously remember it or not.

Sometimes I look at a friend or client and see the little girl or boy they once were. Their laugh, facial expression, or gesture has distinct childish qualities that are unmistakable. Even a person's voice can change from responsible adult to a higher pitched tone and there it is, that innocence.

Alice Miller is one of my heroes. She has written prolifically on the subject of child abuse and how it gets passed down from one generation to the next through cultural and familial denial. She asserts that any individual who has not spent time unearthing the child they once were, coming to understand what it was like to be defenseless and vulnerable, will pass unresolved remembrances onto their children or loved ones. She has made it her life's work to prove that this is so.

"They did the best they could" is a phrase people use to dismiss the betrayals, abandonment, and violations they suffered. They do not want to go back and feel the raw emotion from the past. They believe it is easier to forget. But if you take a good look at someone's life, someone who doesn't want to look into their past, you can usually see the consequences of that choice. They are usually running scared, sprinting as fast as they can from what is screaming the loudest.

How does healing involve the inner child?

In the quiet of a dim-lit room, my lover kisses my neck. I feel aroused and full of love. He touches my arm and tells me he loves me. I brush against his beard and the feel of the coarse hair interrupts my awareness. I am suddenly taken back to a moment with my father when he told me to give him a hug, his beard passing over my cheek. I fall into terror, my heart beating fast, my muscles tensing. I am no longer an adult, I am five years old. I feel small and trapped.

Later, I will write in my journal, let my five year old speak of that moment. I will travel backwards to a very different reality than the life I have created in the present time. My little girl will tell me through feelings and words what it was like to have a Daddy who had no boundaries, who hugged as a way to control, who took from my energy as a source of his own. As I scribble with my pen, I will look out through eyes from thirty-one years ago, breathe from delicate lungs that became asthmatic. I will hold that child, listen to her and I will not tell her she is stupid or lying or overreacting. Eventually, I will discover that she blamed herself for wanting to push him away.

Once I take the time to be five again, to reassess my guilt, to reevaluate my black and white fears, the world will look different to me. I will gaze at my boyfriend, hug him close, feel his beard against my skin, and nothing strange will happen. He will just be my partner, my safe and caring lover. Or maybe I will get scared again, begin to hark back to that belief that men are unsafe. But I have been here before and I understand what it is about. I will remind the child from long ago that it is over, I was not to blame. She will hear me, and relax.

How could God let this happen to me?

Clients have asked me questions such as, "How could God have let my mother leave when I was four years old?" "How could God have left me alone with my stepfather and let him molest me?" "Why did God make the kids at school torment me?" "Where was God when my parents got divorced and I started binge eating?"

Was it God who left you I ask, or was it your mother? Was it God who molested you or was it your stepfather? Did God tease you on the schoolyard or neglect you when your parents got divorced? A thorough examination of these questions allow the client to look at where the hurt, neglect, and abuse came from and it always came down to human fault.

It is a protective act for a child to conclude that God abandoned them rather then feel that their actual mother left them to fend for themselves. How logical it is for a child to think that God came down and violated his or her body rather than to experience the horror of being molested by someone you love who is supposed to keep you safe. Many times, the parent or trusted adult is God in that child's life for they are too innocent to know the difference. To reconcile the human experience of trauma with the existence of a higher power or spiritual force is a journey unto itself.

For me, the visceral connection to spiritual guidance has been the antidote to traumatic programming. I have gone back into memories of getting abused, been catapulted into the blackness and pain, to discover that Spirit was there holding me outside my body. This is how I survived. I've come to understand that people hurt me, and horrible events occurred, but God was the safety there, not the suffering.

How do I heal feeling bad about myself?

Imagine a baby. Imagine telling a baby that he or she is unlovable. Imagine people ignoring the baby, hitting the baby, or holding the baby in an angry and distracted way. The idea of treating a baby like this makes most people cringe. "No," they would tell me, "I would never do that." Yet this is how we treat ourselves. This is what we do to our own innocent, vulnerable, sweet selves.

We tell ourselves that we are ugly, stupid, wrong, disgusting, inadequate, and unlovable. We see ourselves through the hurts of our past when we were rejected or blamed. Even when the people who hurt us are gone, we take over the job and run the tapes of pain without awareness. It is the same as criticizing a baby.

You will not feel good about yourself until you see how criticism works inside of you. You have to make the pattern conscious but don't judge yourself for judging yourself! You just need to notice it, like watching a movie, or listening to a book on tape.

I used to be very anxious when I had time off. I didn't know why, I just noticed that I could not unwind. It wasn't until I slowed down and listened that I could hear my wounded self saying, "You don't deserve time off, you're lazy, everything will fall apart if you relax." I tuned into my guidance and asked if this was true, was it safe to take some down time? Spirit smiled on me and told me I would actually be more productive if I relaxed. That felt true to me and so I followed it. The more I let down, the better it felt. The lie of pushing myself became an echo from long ago and the criticism around this issue eventually lost its power.

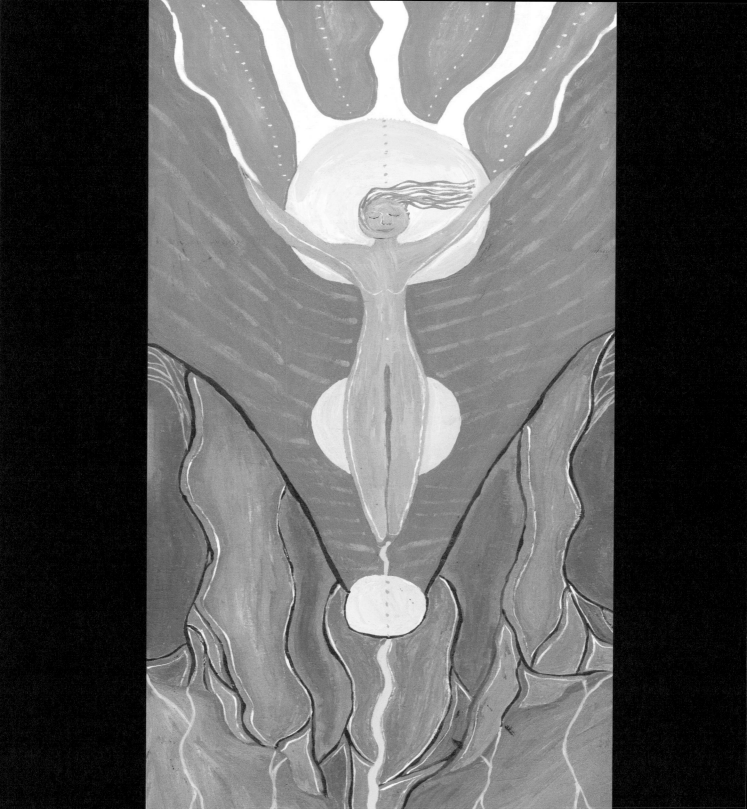

I have heard the phrase "feeling safe" in regard to the healing process, what does that mean?

Children's safety comes from loving adults who protect them and care for their well being. When safety is violated for any reason, the world can come to feel like a minefield for a child, an unpredictable, dangerous environment where relaxation is impossible.

As adults, it is up to us to keep ourselves safe by making boundaries, speaking up, taking care of our bodies and passions. When we betray ourselves by not listening in to what feels safe and good, fear is the result. The child inside continues to feel alone and neglected. There is no trust that an internalized adult is in charge, setting limits, listening to subtle and loud cues from the body, mind, and heart.

People who have not learned how to take care of themselves will relive their unsafe childhood in everyday life. It may seem as if bad things happen for no reason. It may feel as if there is no dependable pathway to another person. This means inner safety has not been created.

"Feeling safe" is the sensation of knowing you will not betray yourself. You will not abandon yourself. You will not turn on yourself or blame yourself. You know you can take care of your needs and that you are co-creating your life with Spirit. You trust that even if scary or unpredictable events occur, you will be loving to yourself. Yes, that's it. The commitment to love and cherish oneself, even in the face of our very wounded world, creates inner safety that is not dependent on external happenings.

Talk about success.

I know a kind of success that is mad. It feeds off my insecurity like a starving animal. It cannot be contained, snickers at my thirst, leaves me drooling. I can trace it back to moments of teenage fantasy when loneliness propelled me to stand in front of my bedroom mirror. I would imagine being a famous movie star or Broadway dancer, adored by droves of people including my parents. These dreams were "success" dreams, transforming my unbearable now into a future of glory. Success dreams were my jelly donuts, my marijuana, my eight mile run. I grew into a success-starved adult who could not be good enough. Each achievement was a point on the scoreboard of a game that would not end. When a performance of my choreography was over, despite applause and effusive compliments, I became bereft. The success could not settle the old wounds, the lack of love from before. I would set out a day later, planning the next show, hoping that this time I would be satisfied.

There is another kind of success that is taking over. I wrote a song at midnight about the man who changed my waking and sleeping world. He stood at the door of my protections, waving at my "No Visitors Allowed" sign. I conjured up lyrics like a sea diver, dipping into quiet depths, discovering just the right poetry to speak my feelings. My fingers toyed with the chords and melodies until a sweet balance of words and sound almost made me squeal. At two in the morning, I was still sitting on my maroon couch, singing the tune over and over. I was alone in my pleasure and utterly fulfilled. It was the kind of success that needs no approval.

Tell me what the payoff is for healing your wounds.

Life is a relentless crash course on fortitude. I planted my feet in the earth of the invisible; my goodness. In each moment of questioning the rational, the pain, the injuries, a funky comic made its way through my eyes. I began to play as a one woman carnival. I made performances dressed in a purple robe, spoke about lust and the boorish weight of the status quo. I became a weird performance artist. People laughed very hard (in a good way). Inside, I knew it was because I dared to inhabit my body and its outrageous victories. I won. I won. Because I believed myself. Because I gave my heartache a vehicle for outrage. Because I didn't pretend it was all fine. Because I wouldn't shut up. Because I wanted to thrive, not wallow. Because if nothing else, I knew how to be honest. Because in the end, I've got me, I've got God, and we've got a good thing going on. Because love is born each moment and without it everything sours. Because art is the

willingness to sign my name on a spot reserved for transfor-
mation. Because I open my doors to other persistent heart-
centered people. Because when we share what is real and
true, it is nothing less than blissful.

What steps can I take to begin healing in a fully committed way?

When a deep internal decision has been made to step into an authentic healing process, then tools for this endeavor are everywhere. You have to be ready to prioritize your healing in order to find them. Still, here are some signposts along the highway to your destination.

1. Find a support person who can witness your thoughts, feelings, and beliefs with true compassion and insight.

2. Keep your eyes and heart open for individuals who seem joyous yet real. Be willing to seek out people who are living healthy lives and taking care of themselves.

3. Tune into your spiritual guidance, whatever that means to you, and begin a two-way dialogue. You can do this through writing, drawing, or talking out loud. Entertain the idea that there is a guide for you who knows all the answers to your big and little questions.

4. Notice how you talk to yourself inside your head. Slow down and hear what you say to yourself all day long. If you find that you are criticizing yourself, recognize the lies and be willing to become the loving parent you have been waiting for.

5. Make healing your pain a priority and take loving action towards that intention such as resting, eating healthy foods, exercising, meditating, or reaching out to friends.

6. Be willing to feel. Watch how you turn to addictions to avoid emotions. Sit still at least once a day and be with the sadness, anger, fear, or shame you might be running from. You could be avoiding joy as well!

7. Find a picture of yourself as a little child. Hang it where you can view it often. Take a moment and see your essence, your goodness, your innocence in that child's eyes. Love begins there.

Any final thoughts or advice about discovering wholeness?

Don't give away your authority. No other person knows what is best for you, who you should love or how. No one but you knows what your work is in the world, your purpose, your passions. At the end of the day, it is you who has to live the life you have created. You have to get up every day and dance inside the choices you have made.

As an adult in this culture, it is so tempting to play safe, to cling to material things and hold them close the way others do. It only takes a moment to stop and tune into your very real and brilliant knowing.

I say, jump off the cliff of your control. Leave it at the shore. Walk with your palms up. Move your hips, and be willing to lose everything. Just to be you in this one life as your unique spirit. What the heck.

You can play it safe. You can hide the pain. You can keep yourself inside the world's approval. But you are much

more than that and you know it. You have so much to say,
feel, express, invent, create, digest, grapple.
Eat it up, you're hungry.

Rythea Lee is a professional dancer and multidisciplinary artist giving voice to personal and global stories of healing. Her dance theater company Zany Angels has spent the last several years performing and teaching workshops at colleges such as Bates College, Sarah Lawrence College, Emerson College, Hampshire College, Mt. Holyoke College, and Smith College. She has collaborated with organizations fighting to end violence against women and children in Massachusetts including Every Womens Center, Safe Passage, The Rape Crisis Center of Central Massachusetts, Hampshire College Health Coalition, and also To Tell the Truth Conference in NYC. She is a graduate of New York University and holds a Masters Degree in Spiritual Psychology. Rythea Lee has a private practice in Northampton, MA as an Inner Bonding® counselor helping people transform trauma, addictions, relationships, and life purpose questions into lasting spiritual and emotional clarity.

Healing Takes Guts! is a workshop based on the material in this book designed for schools, recovery centers, and art-based groups.

Rythea Lee is available for book clubs who are reading her book and would like to do a tele-conference call to meet the author and ask questions.
Please visit www.zanyangels.com or email rythea@crocker.com
To order more of these books, go to:
www.amazon.com or www.barnesandnoble.com

CPSIA information can be obtained
at www.ICGtesting.com
Printed in the USA
BVHW061130120320
574848BV00002B/44